Firearms Inventory Log

owner:

Name: _____

Address: _____

_____

Phone Number: _____

Email Address: _____

Log Start Date: _____

Log End Date: _____

Logbook Number: _____

Notes: _____
_____

Keep this inventory book in a safe place.

Ensure all information is accurate and up to date in case it is needed for police and/or insurance claims. This information may also be needed in the event of the death of the owner, so survivors know the wishes of the owner regarding the disposition of these firearms (check estate law in your jurisdiction.)

The Second Amendment:

A well regulated Militia,

being necessary to the security of a free State,

the right of the people to keep and bear Arms,

shall not be infringed.

Insurance Information

Insurance Company: _____

Policy number: _____

Start date: _____ End date: _____

Policy cost: _____ Coverage type: _____

Insurance agent/contact: _____ Phone number: _____

Email address: _____ Website: _____

Fax number: _____

Notes: _____

_____

_____

_____

Insurance Information

Insurance Company: _____

Policy number: _____

Start date: _____ End date: _____

Policy cost: _____ Coverage type: _____

Insurance agent/contact: _____ Phone number: _____

Email address: _____ Website: _____

Fax number: _____

Notes: _____

_____

_____

_____

Insurance Information

Insurance Company: _____

Policy number: _____

Start date: _____ End date: _____

Policy cost: _____ Coverage type: _____

Insurance agent/contact: _____ Phone number: _____

Email address: _____ Website: _____

Fax number: _____

Notes: _____

_____

_____

_____

Insurance Information

Insurance Company: _____

Policy number: _____

Start date: _____ End date: _____

Policy cost: _____ Coverage type: _____

Insurance agent/contact: _____ Phone number: _____

Email address: _____ Website: _____

Fax number: _____

Notes: _____

_____

_____

_____

Master Index

Firearm Make/Model	Serial Number	Inventory Number	Page Number

Master Index

Firearm Make/Model	Serial Number	Inventory Number	Page Number

Master Index

Firearm Make/Model	Serial Number	Inventory Number	Page Number

FIREARM DETAILS

☐ New   ☐ Used

Make/Manufacturer:		Inventory Number:	
		Serial Number:	
Model:		Firearm Type:	☐ Pistol ☐ Revolver ☐ Rifle ☐ Shotgun ☐ Muzzle loader/black powder ☐ Air gun ☐ Other
Importer:		Barrel Length:	
Caliber/Gauge:		NFA item?	☐ Yes ☐ No
Action:		Curio/Relic?	☐ Yes ☐ No
Weight:		Sights:	
Ammunition Capacity:		Scope/Rings:	
Stock Type:		Stock Material:	
Other Accessories:		Other identifying marks:	
Alterations:			
Repairs:			
Notes:			

In the event of my death, this firearm should go to:

This space for images, sketches, other notes, etc.

ACQUISITION DETAILS

Purchased / Acquired From:		Date:	
Address:			
Phone Number:		Email Address:	
Assessed Value:		Purchase Price:	
Inventory Number:		Condition:	
Other Details:			

DISPOSITION DETAILS

Sold / Traded / Gifted / Disposed of to:		Date:	
Address:			
Phone Number:		Email Address:	
Assessed Value:		Sale Price:	
Inventory Number:		Condition:	
Other Details:			
Lost or stolen? ☐ Yes ☐ No		Date discovered lost/stolen:	
Date reported to police:		Police Case Number:	
Date reported to insurance:		Insurance Claim Number:	

FIREARM DETAILS	☐ New ☐ Used	Inventory Number:	
Make/Manufacturer:		Serial Number:	
Model:		Firearm Type:	☐ Pistol ☐ Revolver ☐ Rifle ☐ Shotgun ☐ Muzzle loader/black powder ☐ Air gun ☐ Other
Importer:		Barrel Length:	
Caliber/Gauge:		NFA item?	☐ Yes ☐ No
Action:		Curio/Relic?	☐ Yes ☐ No
Weight:		Sights:	
Ammunition Capacity:		Scope/Rings:	
Stock Type:		Stock Material:	
Other Accessories:		Other identifying marks:	
Alterations:			
Repairs:			
Notes:			
In the event of my death, this firearm should go to:			

This space for images, sketches, other notes, etc.

ACQUISITION DETAILS

Purchased / Acquired From:		Date:	
Address:			
Phone Number:		Email Address:	
Assessed Value:		Purchase Price:	
Inventory Number:		Condition:	
Other Details:			

DISPOSITION DETAILS

Sold / Traded / Gifted / Disposed of to:		Date:	
Address:			
Phone Number:		Email Address:	
Assessed Value:		Sale Price:	
Inventory Number:		Condition:	
Other Details:			
Lost or stolen? ☐ Yes ☐ No		Date discovered lost/stolen:	
Date reported to police:		Police Case Number:	
Date reported to insurance:		Insurance Claim Number:	

FIREARM DETAILS	☐ New ☐ Used	Inventory Number:	
Make/Manufacturer:		Serial Number:	
Model:		Firearm Type:	☐ Pistol ☐ Revolver ☐ Rifle ☐ Shotgun ☐ Muzzle loader/black powder ☐ Air gun ☐ Other
Importer:		Barrel Length:	
Caliber/Gauge:		NFA item?	☐ Yes ☐ No
Action:		Curio/Relic?	☐ Yes ☐ No
Weight:		Sights:	
Ammunition Capacity:		Scope/Rings:	
Stock Type:		Stock Material:	
Other Accessories:		Other identifying marks:	
Alterations:			
Repairs:			
Notes:			
In the event of my death, this firearm should go to:			

This space for images, sketches, other notes, etc.

ACQUISITION DETAILS

Purchased / Acquired From:		Date:	
Address:			
Phone Number:		Email Address:	
Assessed Value:		Purchase Price:	
Inventory Number:		Condition:	
Other Details:			

DISPOSITION DETAILS

Sold / Traded / Gifted / Disposed of to:		Date:	
Address:			
Phone Number:		Email Address:	
Assessed Value:		Sale Price:	
Inventory Number:		Condition:	
Other Details:			
Lost or stolen? ☐ Yes ☐ No	Date discovered lost/stolen:		
Date reported to police:		Police Case Number:	
Date reported to insurance:		Insurance Claim Number:	

FIREARM DETAILS	☐ New ☐ Used	Inventory Number:	
Make/Manufacturer:		Serial Number:	
Model:		Firearm Type:	☐ Pistol ☐ Revolver ☐ Rifle ☐ Shotgun ☐ Muzzle loader/black powder ☐ Air gun ☐ Other
Importer:		Barrel Length:	
Caliber/Gauge:		NFA item?	☐ Yes ☐ No
Action:		Curio/Relic?	☐ Yes ☐ No
Weight:		Sights:	
Ammunition Capacity:		Scope/Rings:	
Stock Type:		Stock Material:	
Other Accessories:		Other identifying marks:	
Alterations:			
Repairs:			
Notes:			
In the event of my death, this firearm should go to:			

This space for images, sketches, other notes, etc.

ACQUISITION DETAILS

Purchased / Acquired From:		Date:
Address:		
Phone Number:	Email Address:	
Assessed Value:	Purchase Price:	
Inventory Number:	Condition:	
Other Details:		

DISPOSITION DETAILS

Sold / Traded / Gifted / Disposed of to:		Date:
Address:		
Phone Number:	Email Address:	
Assessed Value:	Sale Price:	
Inventory Number:	Condition:	
Other Details:		
Lost or stolen? ☐ Yes ☐ No	Date discovered lost/stolen:	
Date reported to police:	Police Case Number:	
Date reported to insurance:	Insurance Claim Number:	

FIREARM DETAILS

☐ New   ☐ Used

Make/Manufacturer:	
Model:	
Importer:	
Caliber/Gauge:	
Action:	
Weight:	
Ammunition Capacity:	
Stock Type:	
Other Accessories:	
Alterations:	
Repairs:	
Notes:	

Inventory Number:

Serial Number:

Firearm Type:
☐ Pistol   ☐ Revolver
☐ Rifle   ☐ Shotgun
☐ Muzzle loader/black powder
☐ Air gun   ☐ Other

Barrel Length:

NFA item? ☐ Yes   ☐ No

Curio/Relic? ☐ Yes   ☐ No

Sights:

Scope/Rings:

Stock Material:

Other identifying marks:

In the event of my death, this firearm should go to:

This space for images, sketches, other notes, etc.

ACQUISITION DETAILS

Purchased / Acquired From:		Date:
Address:		
Phone Number:	Email Address:	
Assessed Value:	Purchase Price:	
Inventory Number:	Condition:	
Other Details:		

DISPOSITION DETAILS

Sold / Traded / Gifted / Disposed of to:		Date:
Address:		
Phone Number:	Email Address:	
Assessed Value:	Sale Price:	
Inventory Number:	Condition:	
Other Details:		
Lost or stolen? ☐ Yes ☐ No	Date discovered lost/stolen:	
Date reported to police:	Police Case Number:	
Date reported to insurance:	Insurance Claim Number:	

FIREARM DETAILS ☐ New ☐ Used		Inventory Number:	
Make/Manufacturer:		Serial Number:	
Model:		Firearm Type:	☐ Pistol ☐ Revolver ☐ Rifle ☐ Shotgun ☐ Muzzle loader/black powder ☐ Air gun ☐ Other
Importer:		Barrel Length:	
Caliber/Gauge:		NFA item?	☐ Yes ☐ No
Action:		Curio/Relic?	☐ Yes ☐ No
Weight:		Sights:	
Ammunition Capacity:		Scope/Rings:	
Stock Type:		Stock Material:	
Other Accessories:		Other identifying marks:	
Alterations:			
Repairs:			
Notes:			
In the event of my death, this firearm should go to:			

This space for images, sketches, other notes, etc.

ACQUISITION DETAILS

Purchased / Acquired From:		Date:	
Address:			
Phone Number:		Email Address:	
Assessed Value:		Purchase Price:	
Inventory Number:		Condition:	
Other Details:			

DISPOSITION DETAILS

Sold / Traded / Gifted / Disposed of to:		Date:	
Address:			
Phone Number:		Email Address:	
Assessed Value:		Sale Price:	
Inventory Number:		Condition:	
Other Details:			
Lost or stolen? ☐ Yes ☐ No	Date discovered lost/stolen:		
Date reported to police:		Police Case Number:	
Date reported to insurance:		Insurance Claim Number:	

FIREARM DETAILS	☐ New ☐ Used	Inventory Number:	
Make/Manufacturer:		Serial Number:	
Model:		Firearm Type:	☐ Pistol ☐ Revolver ☐ Rifle ☐ Shotgun ☐ Muzzle loader/black powder ☐ Air gun ☐ Other
Importer:		Barrel Length:	
Caliber/Gauge:		NFA item?	☐ Yes ☐ No
Action:		Curio/Relic?	☐ Yes ☐ No
Weight:		Sights:	
Ammunition Capacity:		Scope/Rings:	
Stock Type:		Stock Material:	
Other Accessories:		Other identifying marks:	
Alterations:			
Repairs:			
Notes:			
In the event of my death, this firearm should go to:			

This space for images, sketches, other notes, etc.

ACQUISITION DETAILS

Purchased / Acquired From:		Date:	
Address:			
Phone Number:		Email Address:	
Assessed Value:		Purchase Price:	
Inventory Number:		Condition:	
Other Details:			

DISPOSITION DETAILS

Sold / Traded / Gifted / Disposed of to:		Date:	
Address:			
Phone Number:		Email Address:	
Assessed Value:		Sale Price:	
Inventory Number:		Condition:	
Other Details:			
Lost or stolen? ☐ Yes ☐ No	Date discovered lost/stolen:		
Date reported to police:		Police Case Number:	
Date reported to insurance:		Insurance Claim Number:	

FIREARM DETAILS	☐ New ☐ Used	Inventory Number:	
Make/Manufacturer:		Serial Number:	
Model:		Firearm Type:	☐ Pistol ☐ Revolver ☐ Rifle ☐ Shotgun ☐ Muzzle loader/black powder ☐ Air gun ☐ Other
Importer:		Barrel Length:	
Caliber/Gauge:		NFA item?	☐ Yes ☐ No
Action:		Curio/Relic?	☐ Yes ☐ No
Weight:		Sights:	
Ammunition Capacity:		Scope/Rings:	
Stock Type:		Stock Material:	
Other Accessories:		Other identifying marks:	
Alterations:			
Repairs:			
Notes:			
In the event of my death, this firearm should go to:			

This space for images, sketches, other notes, etc.

ACQUISITION DETAILS

Purchased / Acquired From:		Date:
Address:		
Phone Number:		Email Address:
Assessed Value:		Purchase Price:
Inventory Number:		Condition:
Other Details:		

DISPOSITION DETAILS

Sold / Traded / Gifted / Disposed of to:		Date:
Address:		
Phone Number:		Email Address:
Assessed Value:		Sale Price:
Inventory Number:		Condition:
Other Details:		
Lost or stolen? ☐ Yes ☐ No	Date discovered lost/stolen:	
Date reported to police:		Police Case Number:
Date reported to insurance:		Insurance Claim Number:

FIREARM DETAILS

☐ New ☐ Used

Make/Manufacturer:	
Model:	
Importer:	
Caliber/Gauge:	
Action:	
Weight:	
Ammunition Capacity:	
Stock Type:	
Other Accessories:	
Alterations:	
Repairs:	
Notes:	

Inventory Number:	
Serial Number:	
Firearm Type:	☐ Pistol ☐ Revolver ☐ Rifle ☐ Shotgun ☐ Muzzle loader/black powder ☐ Air gun ☐ Other
Barrel Length:	
NFA item?	☐ Yes ☐ No
Curio/Relic?	☐ Yes ☐ No
Sights:	
Scope/Rings:	
Stock Material:	
Other identifying marks:	

In the event of my death, this firearm should go to:

This space for images, sketches, other notes, etc.

ACQUISITION DETAILS

Purchased / Acquired From:		Date:	
Address:			
Phone Number:		Email Address:	
Assessed Value:		Purchase Price:	
Inventory Number:		Condition:	
Other Details:			

DISPOSITION DETAILS

Sold / Traded / Gifted / Disposed of to:		Date:	
Address:			
Phone Number:		Email Address:	
Assessed Value:		Sale Price:	
Inventory Number:		Condition:	
Other Details:			
Lost or stolen? ☐ Yes ☐ No		Date discovered lost/stolen:	
Date reported to police:		Police Case Number:	
Date reported to insurance:		Insurance Claim Number:	

FIREARM DETAILS	☐ New ☐ Used	Inventory Number:	
Make/Manufacturer:		Serial Number:	
Model:		Firearm Type:	☐ Pistol ☐ Revolver ☐ Rifle ☐ Shotgun ☐ Muzzle loader/black powder ☐ Air gun ☐ Other
Importer:		Barrel Length:	
Caliber/Gauge:		NFA item?	☐ Yes ☐ No
Action:		Curio/Relic?	☐ Yes ☐ No
Weight:		Sights:	
Ammunition Capacity:		Scope/Rings:	
Stock Type:		Stock Material:	
Other Accessories:		Other identifying marks:	
Alterations:			
Repairs:			
Notes:			
In the event of my death, this firearm should go to:			

This space for images, sketches, other notes, etc.

26

ACQUISITION DETAILS

Purchased / Acquired From:		Date:	
Address:			
Phone Number:		Email Address:	
Assessed Value:		Purchase Price:	
Inventory Number:		Condition:	
Other Details:			

DISPOSITION DETAILS

Sold / Traded / Gifted / Disposed of to:		Date:	
Address:			
Phone Number:		Email Address:	
Assessed Value:		Sale Price:	
Inventory Number:		Condition:	
Other Details:			
Lost or stolen? ☐ Yes ☐ No		Date discovered lost/stolen:	
Date reported to police:		Police Case Number:	
Date reported to insurance:		Insurance Claim Number:	

FIREARM DETAILS

☐ New   ☐ Used

Make/Manufacturer:		Inventory Number:	
Model:		Serial Number:	
		Firearm Type:	☐ Pistol ☐ Revolver ☐ Rifle ☐ Shotgun ☐ Muzzle loader/black powder ☐ Air gun ☐ Other
Importer:		Barrel Length:	
Caliber/Gauge:		NFA item?	☐ Yes ☐ No
Action:		Curio/Relic?	☐ Yes ☐ No
Weight:		Sights:	
Ammunition Capacity:		Scope/Rings:	
Stock Type:		Stock Material:	
Other Accessories:		Other identifying marks:	
Alterations:			
Repairs:			
Notes:			

In the event of my death, this firearm should go to:

This space for images, sketches, other notes, etc.

ACQUISITION DETAILS

Purchased / Acquired From:		Date:
Address:		
Phone Number:	Email Address:	
Assessed Value:	Purchase Price:	
Inventory Number:	Condition:	
Other Details:		

DISPOSITION DETAILS

Sold / Traded / Gifted / Disposed of to:		Date:
Address:		
Phone Number:	Email Address:	
Assessed Value:	Sale Price:	
Inventory Number:	Condition:	
Other Details:		
Lost or stolen? ☐ Yes ☐ No	Date discovered lost/stolen:	
Date reported to police:	Police Case Number:	
Date reported to insurance:	Insurance Claim Number:	

FIREARM DETAILS	☐ New ☐ Used	Inventory Number:	
Make/Manufacturer:		Serial Number:	
Model:		Firearm Type:	☐ Pistol ☐ Revolver ☐ Rifle ☐ Shotgun ☐ Muzzle loader/black powder ☐ Air gun ☐ Other
Importer:		Barrel Length:	
Caliber/Gauge:		NFA item?	☐ Yes ☐ No
Action:		Curio/Relic?	☐ Yes ☐ No
Weight:		Sights:	
Ammunition Capacity:		Scope/Rings:	
Stock Type:		Stock Material:	
Other Accessories:		Other identifying marks:	
Alterations:			
Repairs:			
Notes:			
In the event of my death, this firearm should go to:			

This space for images, sketches, other notes, etc.

ACQUISITION DETAILS

Purchased / Acquired From:		Date:	
Address:			
Phone Number:		Email Address:	
Assessed Value:		Purchase Price:	
Inventory Number:		Condition:	
Other Details:			

DISPOSITION DETAILS

Sold / Traded / Gifted / Disposed of to:		Date:	
Address:			
Phone Number:		Email Address:	
Assessed Value:		Sale Price:	
Inventory Number:		Condition:	
Other Details:			

Lost or stolen? ☐ Yes ☐ No	Date discovered lost/stolen:	
Date reported to police:	Police Case Number:	
Date reported to insurance:	Insurance Claim Number:	

FIREARM DETAILS	☐ New ☐ Used	Inventory Number:	
Make/Manufacturer:		Serial Number:	
Model:		Firearm Type:	☐ Pistol ☐ Revolver ☐ Rifle ☐ Shotgun ☐ Muzzle loader/black powder ☐ Air gun ☐ Other
Importer:		Barrel Length:	
Caliber/Gauge:		NFA item?	☐ Yes ☐ No
Action:		Curio/Relic?	☐ Yes ☐ No
Weight:		Sights:	
Ammunition Capacity:		Scope/Rings:	
Stock Type:		Stock Material:	
Other Accessories:		Other identifying marks:	
Alterations:			
Repairs:			
Notes:			
In the event of my death, this firearm should go to:			

This space for images, sketches, other notes, etc.

ACQUISITION DETAILS

Purchased / Acquired From:		Date:
Address:		
Phone Number:	Email Address:	
Assessed Value:	Purchase Price:	
Inventory Number:	Condition:	
Other Details:		

DISPOSITION DETAILS

Sold / Traded / Gifted / Disposed of to:		Date:
Address:		
Phone Number:	Email Address:	
Assessed Value:	Sale Price:	
Inventory Number:	Condition:	
Other Details:		
Lost or stolen? ☐ Yes ☐ No	Date discovered lost/stolen:	
Date reported to police:	Police Case Number:	
Date reported to insurance:	Insurance Claim Number:	

FIREARM DETAILS

☐ New   ☐ Used   Inventory Number:

Make/Manufacturer:		Serial Number:	
Model:		Firearm Type:	☐ Pistol ☐ Revolver ☐ Rifle ☐ Shotgun ☐ Muzzle loader/black powder ☐ Air gun ☐ Other
Importer:		Barrel Length:	
Caliber/Gauge:		NFA item?	☐ Yes ☐ No
Action:		Curio/Relic?	☐ Yes ☐ No
Weight:		Sights:	
Ammunition Capacity:		Scope/Rings:	
Stock Type:		Stock Material:	
Other Accessories:		Other identifying marks:	
Alterations:			
Repairs:			
Notes:			

In the event of my death, this firearm should go to:

This space for images, sketches, other notes, etc.

ACQUISITION DETAILS

Purchased / Acquired From:		Date:
Address:		
Phone Number:		Email Address:
Assessed Value:		Purchase Price:
Inventory Number:		Condition:
Other Details:		

DISPOSITION DETAILS

Sold / Traded / Gifted / Disposed of to:		Date:
Address:		
Phone Number:		Email Address:
Assessed Value:		Sale Price:
Inventory Number:		Condition:
Other Details:		

Lost or stolen? ☐ Yes ☐ No

Date discovered lost/stolen:	
Date reported to police:	Police Case Number:
Date reported to insurance:	Insurance Claim Number:

FIREARM DETAILS

☐ New   ☐ Used

		Inventory Number:	
Make/Manufacturer:		Serial Number:	
Model:		Firearm Type:	☐ Pistol ☐ Revolver ☐ Rifle ☐ Shotgun ☐ Muzzle loader/black powder ☐ Air gun ☐ Other
Importer:		Barrel Length:	
Caliber/Gauge:		NFA item?	☐ Yes ☐ No
Action:		Curio/Relic?	☐ Yes ☐ No
Weight:		Sights:	
Ammunition Capacity:		Scope/Rings:	
Stock Type:		Stock Material:	
Other Accessories:		Other identifying marks:	
Alterations:			
Repairs:			
Notes:			

In the event of my death, this firearm should go to:

This space for images, sketches, other notes, etc.

ACQUISITION DETAILS

Purchased / Acquired From:		Date:
Address:		
Phone Number:	Email Address:	
Assessed Value:	Purchase Price:	
Inventory Number:	Condition:	
Other Details:		

DISPOSITION DETAILS

Sold / Traded / Gifted / Disposed of to:		Date:
Address:		
Phone Number:	Email Address:	
Assessed Value:	Sale Price:	
Inventory Number:	Condition:	
Other Details:		
Lost or stolen? ☐ Yes ☐ No	Date discovered lost/stolen:	
Date reported to police:	Police Case Number:	
Date reported to insurance:	Insurance Claim Number:	

FIREARM DETAILS	☐ New	☐ Used	Inventory Number:	
Make/Manufacturer:			Serial Number:	
Model:			Firearm Type:	☐ Pistol ☐ Revolver ☐ Rifle ☐ Shotgun ☐ Muzzle loader/black powder ☐ Air gun ☐ Other
Importer:			Barrel Length:	
Caliber/Gauge:			NFA item?	☐ Yes ☐ No
Action:			Curio/Relic?	☐ Yes ☐ No
Weight:			Sights:	
Ammunition Capacity:			Scope/Rings:	
Stock Type:			Stock Material:	
Other Accessories:			Other identifying marks:	
Alterations:				
Repairs:				
Notes:				
In the event of my death, this firearm should go to:				

This space for images, sketches, other notes, etc.

ACQUISITION DETAILS

Purchased / Acquired From:		Date:
Address:		
Phone Number:		Email Address:
Assessed Value:		Purchase Price:
Inventory Number:		Condition:
Other Details:		

DISPOSITION DETAILS

Sold / Traded / Gifted / Disposed of to:		Date:
Address:		
Phone Number:		Email Address:
Assessed Value:		Sale Price:
Inventory Number:		Condition:
Other Details:		

Lost or stolen? ☐ Yes ☐ No	Date discovered lost/stolen:	
Date reported to police:		Police Case Number:
Date reported to insurance:		Insurance Claim Number:

FIREARM DETAILS	☐ New ☐ Used	Inventory Number:	
Make/Manufacturer:		Serial Number:	
Model:		Firearm Type:	☐ Pistol ☐ Revolver ☐ Rifle ☐ Shotgun ☐ Muzzle loader/black powder ☐ Air gun ☐ Other
Importer:		Barrel Length:	
Caliber/Gauge:		NFA item?	☐ Yes ☐ No
Action:		Curio/Relic?	☐ Yes ☐ No
Weight:		Sights:	
Ammunition Capacity:		Scope/Rings:	
Stock Type:		Stock Material:	
Other Accessories:		Other identifying marks:	
Alterations:			
Repairs:			
Notes:			
In the event of my death, this firearm should go to:			

This space for images, sketches, other notes, etc.

ACQUISITION DETAILS

Purchased / Acquired From:		Date:
Address:		
Phone Number:		Email Address:
Assessed Value:		Purchase Price:
Inventory Number:		Condition:
Other Details:		

DISPOSITION DETAILS

Sold / Traded / Gifted / Disposed of to:		Date:
Address:		
Phone Number:		Email Address:
Assessed Value:		Sale Price:
Inventory Number:		Condition:
Other Details:		

Lost or stolen? ☐ Yes ☐ No

Date discovered lost/stolen:	
Date reported to police:	Police Case Number:
Date reported to insurance:	Insurance Claim Number:

FIREARM DETAILS

☐ New ☐ Used

Make/Manufacturer:		**Inventory Number:**	
		Serial Number:	
Model:		**Firearm Type:**	☐ Pistol ☐ Revolver ☐ Rifle ☐ Shotgun ☐ Muzzle loader/black powder ☐ Air gun ☐ Other
Importer:		**Barrel Length:**	
Caliber/Gauge:		**NFA item?**	☐ Yes ☐ No
Action:		**Curio/Relic?**	☐ Yes ☐ No
Weight:		**Sights:**	
Ammunition Capacity:		**Scope/Rings:**	
Stock Type:		**Stock Material:**	
Other Accessories:		**Other identifying marks:**	
Alterations:			
Repairs:			
Notes:			
In the event of my death, this firearm should go to:			

This space for images, sketches, other notes, etc.

ACQUISITION DETAILS

Purchased / Acquired From:		**Date:**	
Address:			
Phone Number:		**Email Address:**	
Assessed Value:		**Purchase Price:**	
Inventory Number:		**Condition:**	
Other Details:			

DISPOSITION DETAILS

Sold / Traded / Gifted / Disposed of to:		**Date:**	
Address:			
Phone Number:		**Email Address:**	
Assessed Value:		**Sale Price:**	
Inventory Number:		**Condition:**	
Other Details:			
Lost or stolen? ☐ Yes ☐ No		**Date discovered lost/stolen:**	
Date reported to police:		**Police Case Number:**	
Date reported to insurance:		**Insurance Claim Number:**	

FIREARM DETAILS	☐ New	☐ Used	Inventory Number:	
Make/Manufacturer:			Serial Number:	
Model:			Firearm Type:	☐ Pistol ☐ Revolver ☐ Rifle ☐ Shotgun ☐ Muzzle loader/black powder ☐ Air gun ☐ Other
Importer:			Barrel Length:	
Caliber/Gauge:			NFA item?	☐ Yes ☐ No
Action:			Curio/Relic?	☐ Yes ☐ No
Weight:			Sights:	
Ammunition Capacity:			Scope/Rings:	
Stock Type:			Stock Material:	
Other Accessories:			Other identifying marks:	
Alterations:				
Repairs:				
Notes:				
In the event of my death, this firearm should go to:				

This space for images, sketches, other notes, etc.

ACQUISITION DETAILS

Purchased / Acquired From:		Date:
Address:		
Phone Number:	Email Address:	
Assessed Value:	Purchase Price:	
Inventory Number:	Condition:	
Other Details:		

DISPOSITION DETAILS

Sold / Traded / Gifted / Disposed of to:		Date:
Address:		
Phone Number:	Email Address:	
Assessed Value:	Sale Price:	
Inventory Number:	Condition:	
Other Details:		
Lost or stolen? ☐ Yes ☐ No	Date discovered lost/stolen:	
Date reported to police:	Police Case Number:	
Date reported to insurance:	Insurance Claim Number:	

FIREARM DETAILS

☐ New   ☐ Used

Make/Manufacturer:	
Model:	
Importer:	
Caliber/Gauge:	
Action:	
Weight:	
Ammunition Capacity:	
Stock Type:	
Other Accessories:	
Alterations:	
Repairs:	
Notes:	

Inventory Number:

Serial Number:	
Firearm Type:	☐ Pistol ☐ Revolver ☐ Rifle ☐ Shotgun ☐ Muzzle loader/black powder ☐ Air gun ☐ Other
Barrel Length:	
NFA item?	☐ Yes ☐ No
Curio/Relic?	☐ Yes ☐ No
Sights:	
Scope/Rings:	
Stock Material:	
Other identifying marks:	

In the event of my death, this firearm should go to:

This space for images, sketches, other notes, etc.

ACQUISITION DETAILS

Purchased / Acquired From:		**Date:**
Address:		
Phone Number:		**Email Address:**
Assessed Value:		**Purchase Price:**
Inventory Number:		**Condition:**
Other Details:		

DISPOSITION DETAILS

Sold / Traded / Gifted / Disposed of to:		**Date:**
Address:		
Phone Number:		**Email Address:**
Assessed Value:		**Sale Price:**
Inventory Number:		**Condition:**
Other Details:		
Lost or stolen? ☐ Yes ☐ No	**Date discovered lost/stolen:**	
Date reported to police:		**Police Case Number:**
Date reported to insurance:		**Insurance Claim Number:**

FIREARM DETAILS

☐ New   ☐ Used

Make/Manufacturer:	
Model:	
Importer:	
Caliber/Gauge:	
Action:	
Weight:	
Ammunition Capacity:	
Stock Type:	
Other Accessories:	
Alterations:	
Repairs:	
Notes:	

Inventory Number:

Serial Number:	
Firearm Type:	☐ Pistol ☐ Revolver ☐ Rifle ☐ Shotgun ☐ Muzzle loader/black powder ☐ Air gun ☐ Other
Barrel Length:	
NFA item?	☐ Yes ☐ No
Curio/Relic?	☐ Yes ☐ No
Sights:	
Scope/Rings:	
Stock Material:	
Other identifying marks:	

In the event of my death, this firearm should go to:

This space for images, sketches, other notes, etc.

ACQUISITION DETAILS

Purchased / Acquired From:			Date:	
Address:				
Phone Number:		Email Address:		
Assessed Value:		Purchase Price:		
Inventory Number:		Condition:		
Other Details:				

DISPOSITION DETAILS

Sold / Traded / Gifted / Disposed of to:			Date:	
Address:				
Phone Number:		Email Address:		
Assessed Value:		Sale Price:		
Inventory Number:		Condition:		
Other Details:				

Lost or stolen? ☐ Yes ☐ No	Date discovered lost/stolen:	
Date reported to police:		Police Case Number:
Date reported to insurance:		Insurance Claim Number:

FIREARM DETAILS	☐ New ☐ Used	Inventory Number:		
Make/Manufacturer:		Serial Number:		
Model:		Firearm Type:	☐ Pistol ☐ Revolver ☐ Rifle ☐ Shotgun ☐ Muzzle loader/black powder ☐ Air gun ☐ Other	
Importer:		Barrel Length:		
Caliber/Gauge:		NFA item?	☐ Yes ☐ No	
Action:		Curio/Relic?	☐ Yes ☐ No	
Weight:		Sights:		
Ammunition Capacity:		Scope/Rings:		
Stock Type:		Stock Material:		
Other Accessories:		Other identifying marks:		
Alterations:				
Repairs:				
Notes:				
In the event of my death, this firearm should go to:				

This space for images, sketches, other notes, etc.

ACQUISITION DETAILS

Purchased / Acquired From:		Date:	
Address:			
Phone Number:		Email Address:	
Assessed Value:		Purchase Price:	
Inventory Number:		Condition:	
Other Details:			

DISPOSITION DETAILS

Sold / Traded / Gifted / Disposed of to:		Date:	
Address:			
Phone Number:		Email Address:	
Assessed Value:		Sale Price:	
Inventory Number:		Condition:	
Other Details:			
Lost or stolen? ☐ Yes ☐ No		Date discovered lost/stolen:	
Date reported to police:		Police Case Number:	
Date reported to insurance:		Insurance Claim Number:	

FIREARM DETAILS

☐ New   ☐ Used

Make/Manufacturer:		**Inventory Number:**	
		Serial Number:	
Model:		**Firearm Type:**	☐ Pistol ☐ Revolver ☐ Rifle ☐ Shotgun ☐ Muzzle loader/black powder ☐ Air gun ☐ Other
Importer:		**Barrel Length:**	
Caliber/Gauge:		**NFA item?**	☐ Yes ☐ No
Action:		**Curio/Relic?**	☐ Yes ☐ No
Weight:		**Sights:**	
Ammunition Capacity:		**Scope/Rings:**	
Stock Type:		**Stock Material:**	
Other Accessories:		**Other identifying marks:**	
Alterations:			
Repairs:			
Notes:			

In the event of my death, this firearm should go to:	

This space for images, sketches, other notes, etc.

ACQUISITION DETAILS

Purchased / Acquired From:		Date:	
Address:			
Phone Number:		Email Address:	
Assessed Value:		Purchase Price:	
Inventory Number:		Condition:	
Other Details:			

DISPOSITION DETAILS

Sold / Traded / Gifted / Disposed of to:		Date:	
Address:			
Phone Number:		Email Address:	
Assessed Value:		Sale Price:	
Inventory Number:		Condition:	
Other Details:			

Lost or stolen? ☐ Yes ☐ No	Date discovered lost/stolen:	
Date reported to police:		Police Case Number:
Date reported to insurance:		Insurance Claim Number:

FIREARM DETAILS	☐ New ☐ Used	Inventory Number:	
Make/Manufacturer:		Serial Number:	
Model:		Firearm Type:	☐ Pistol ☐ Revolver ☐ Rifle ☐ Shotgun ☐ Muzzle loader/black powder ☐ Air gun ☐ Other
Importer:		Barrel Length:	
Caliber/Gauge:		NFA item?	☐ Yes ☐ No
Action:		Curio/Relic?	☐ Yes ☐ No
Weight:		Sights:	
Ammunition Capacity:		Scope/Rings:	
Stock Type:		Stock Material:	
Other Accessories:		Other identifying marks:	
Alterations:			
Repairs:			
Notes:			
In the event of my death, this firearm should go to:			

This space for images, sketches, other notes, etc.

ACQUISITION DETAILS

Purchased / Acquired From:		Date:
Address:		
Phone Number:	Email Address:	
Assessed Value:	Purchase Price:	
Inventory Number:	Condition:	
Other Details:		

DISPOSITION DETAILS

Sold / Traded / Gifted / Disposed of to:		Date:
Address:		
Phone Number:	Email Address:	
Assessed Value:	Sale Price:	
Inventory Number:	Condition:	
Other Details:		
Lost or stolen? ☐ Yes ☐ No	Date discovered lost/stolen:	
Date reported to police:	Police Case Number:	
Date reported to insurance:	Insurance Claim Number:	

FIREARM DETAILS	☐ New ☐ Used	Inventory Number:	
Make/Manufacturer:		Serial Number:	
Model:		Firearm Type:	☐ Pistol ☐ Revolver ☐ Rifle ☐ Shotgun ☐ Muzzle loader/black powder ☐ Air gun ☐ Other
Importer:		Barrel Length:	
Caliber/Gauge:		NFA item?	☐ Yes ☐ No
Action:		Curio/Relic?	☐ Yes ☐ No
Weight:		Sights:	
Ammunition Capacity:		Scope/Rings:	
Stock Type:		Stock Material:	
Other Accessories:		Other identifying marks:	
Alterations:			
Repairs:			
Notes:			
In the event of my death, this firearm should go to:			

This space for images, sketches, other notes, etc.

ACQUISITION DETAILS

Purchased / Acquired From:		**Date:**
Address:		
Phone Number:	**Email Address:**	
Assessed Value:	**Purchase Price:**	
Inventory Number:	**Condition:**	
Other Details:		

DISPOSITION DETAILS

Sold / Traded / Gifted / Disposed of to:		**Date:**
Address:		
Phone Number:	**Email Address:**	
Assessed Value:	**Sale Price:**	
Inventory Number:	**Condition:**	
Other Details:		
Lost or stolen? ☐ Yes ☐ No	**Date discovered lost/stolen:**	
Date reported to police:	**Police Case Number:**	
Date reported to insurance:	**Insurance Claim Number:**	

FIREARM DETAILS	☐ New ☐ Used	Inventory Number:	
Make/Manufacturer:		Serial Number:	
Model:		Firearm Type:	☐ Pistol ☐ Revolver ☐ Rifle ☐ Shotgun ☐ Muzzle loader/black powder ☐ Air gun ☐ Other
Importer:		Barrel Length:	
Caliber/Gauge:		NFA item?	☐ Yes ☐ No
Action:		Curio/Relic?	☐ Yes ☐ No
Weight:		Sights:	
Ammunition Capacity:		Scope/Rings:	
Stock Type:		Stock Material:	
Other Accessories:		Other identifying marks:	
Alterations:			
Repairs:			
Notes:			
In the event of my death, this firearm should go to:			

This space for images, sketches, other notes, etc.

ACQUISITION DETAILS

Purchased / Acquired From:		Date:
Address:		
Phone Number:		Email Address:
Assessed Value:		Purchase Price:
Inventory Number:		Condition:
Other Details:		

DISPOSITION DETAILS

Sold / Traded / Gifted / Disposed of to:		Date:
Address:		
Phone Number:		Email Address:
Assessed Value:		Sale Price:
Inventory Number:		Condition:
Other Details:		
Lost or stolen? ☐ Yes ☐ No	Date discovered lost/stolen:	
Date reported to police:		Police Case Number:
Date reported to insurance:		Insurance Claim Number:

FIREARM DETAILS

☐ New   ☐ Used

Make/Manufacturer:		**Serial Number:**	
Model:		**Firearm Type:**	☐ Pistol ☐ Revolver ☐ Rifle ☐ Shotgun ☐ Muzzle loader/black powder ☐ Air gun ☐ Other
Importer:		**Barrel Length:**	
Caliber/Gauge:		**NFA item?**	☐ Yes ☐ No
Action:		**Curio/Relic?**	☐ Yes ☐ No
Weight:		**Sights:**	
Ammunition Capacity:		**Scope/Rings:**	
Stock Type:		**Stock Material:**	
Other Accessories:		**Other identifying marks:**	
Alterations:			
Repairs:			
Notes:			

Inventory Number:

In the event of my death, this firearm should go to:

This space for images, sketches, other notes, etc.

ACQUISITION DETAILS

Purchased / Acquired From:		Date:	
Address:			
Phone Number:		Email Address:	
Assessed Value:		Purchase Price:	
Inventory Number:		Condition:	
Other Details:			

DISPOSITION DETAILS

Sold / Traded / Gifted / Disposed of to:		Date:	
Address:			
Phone Number:		Email Address:	
Assessed Value:		Sale Price:	
Inventory Number:		Condition:	
Other Details:			
Lost or stolen? ☐ Yes ☐ No	Date discovered lost/stolen:		
Date reported to police:		Police Case Number:	
Date reported to insurance:		Insurance Claim Number:	

FIREARM DETAILS

☐ New ☐ Used

		Inventory Number:	
Make/Manufacturer:		Serial Number:	
Model:		Firearm Type:	☐ Pistol ☐ Revolver ☐ Rifle ☐ Shotgun ☐ Muzzle loader/black powder ☐ Air gun ☐ Other
Importer:		Barrel Length:	
Caliber/Gauge:		NFA item?	☐ Yes ☐ No
Action:		Curio/Relic?	☐ Yes ☐ No
Weight:		Sights:	
Ammunition Capacity:		Scope/Rings:	
Stock Type:		Stock Material:	
Other Accessories:		Other identifying marks:	
Alterations:			
Repairs:			
Notes:			
In the event of my death, this firearm should go to:			

This space for images, sketches, other notes, etc.

ACQUISITION DETAILS

Purchased / Acquired From:		Date:	
Address:			
Phone Number:		Email Address:	
Assessed Value:		Purchase Price:	
Inventory Number:		Condition:	
Other Details:			

DISPOSITION DETAILS

Sold / Traded / Gifted / Disposed of to:		Date:	
Address:			
Phone Number:		Email Address:	
Assessed Value:		Sale Price:	
Inventory Number:		Condition:	
Other Details:			
Lost or stolen? ☐ Yes ☐ No	Date discovered lost/stolen:		
Date reported to police:		Police Case Number:	
Date reported to insurance:		Insurance Claim Number:	

FIREARM DETAILS	☐ New ☐ Used	Inventory Number:	
Make/Manufacturer:		Serial Number:	
Model:		Firearm Type:	☐ Pistol ☐ Revolver ☐ Rifle ☐ Shotgun ☐ Muzzle loader/black powder ☐ Air gun ☐ Other
Importer:		Barrel Length:	
Caliber/Gauge:		NFA item?	☐ Yes ☐ No
Action:		Curio/Relic?	☐ Yes ☐ No
Weight:		Sights:	
Ammunition Capacity:		Scope/Rings:	
Stock Type:		Stock Material:	
Other Accessories:		Other identifying marks:	
Alterations:			
Repairs:			
Notes:			
In the event of my death, this firearm should go to:			

This space for images, sketches, other notes, etc.

ACQUISITION DETAILS

Purchased / Acquired From:		Date:	
Address:			
Phone Number:		Email Address:	
Assessed Value:		Purchase Price:	
Inventory Number:		Condition:	
Other Details:			

DISPOSITION DETAILS

Sold / Traded / Gifted / Disposed of to:		Date:	
Address:			
Phone Number:		Email Address:	
Assessed Value:		Sale Price:	
Inventory Number:		Condition:	
Other Details:			
Lost or stolen? ☐ Yes ☐ No	Date discovered lost/stolen:		
Date reported to police:		Police Case Number:	
Date reported to insurance:		Insurance Claim Number:	

FIREARM DETAILS

☐ New ☐ Used	Inventory Number:

Make/Manufacturer:		Serial Number:	
Model:		Firearm Type:	☐ Pistol ☐ Revolver ☐ Rifle ☐ Shotgun ☐ Muzzle loader/black powder ☐ Air gun ☐ Other
Importer:		Barrel Length:	
Caliber/Gauge:		NFA item?	☐ Yes ☐ No
Action:		Curio/Relic?	☐ Yes ☐ No
Weight:		Sights:	
Ammunition Capacity:		Scope/Rings:	
Stock Type:		Stock Material:	
Other Accessories:		Other identifying marks:	
Alterations:			
Repairs:			
Notes:			

In the event of my death, this firearm should go to:	

This space for images, sketches, other notes, etc.

ACQUISITION DETAILS

Purchased / Acquired From:		Date:	
Address:			
Phone Number:		Email Address:	
Assessed Value:		Purchase Price:	
Inventory Number:		Condition:	
Other Details:			

DISPOSITION DETAILS

Sold / Traded / Gifted / Disposed of to:		Date:	
Address:			
Phone Number:		Email Address:	
Assessed Value:		Sale Price:	
Inventory Number:		Condition:	
Other Details:			
Lost or stolen? ☐ Yes ☐ No		Date discovered lost/stolen:	
Date reported to police:		Police Case Number:	
Date reported to insurance:		Insurance Claim Number:	

FIREARM DETAILS ☐ New ☐ Used		Inventory Number:	
Make/Manufacturer:		Serial Number:	
Model:		Firearm Type:	☐ Pistol ☐ Revolver ☐ Rifle ☐ Shotgun ☐ Muzzle loader/black powder ☐ Air gun ☐ Other
Importer:		Barrel Length:	
Caliber/Gauge:		NFA item?	☐ Yes ☐ No
Action:		Curio/Relic?	☐ Yes ☐ No
Weight:		Sights:	
Ammunition Capacity:		Scope/Rings:	
Stock Type:		Stock Material:	
Other Accessories:		Other identifying marks:	
Alterations:			
Repairs:			
Notes:			
In the event of my death, this firearm should go to:			

This space for images, sketches, other notes, etc.

ACQUISITION DETAILS

Purchased / Acquired From:		**Date:**	
Address:			
Phone Number:		**Email Address:**	
Assessed Value:		**Purchase Price:**	
Inventory Number:		**Condition:**	
Other Details:			

DISPOSITION DETAILS

Sold / Traded / Gifted / Disposed of to:		**Date:**	
Address:			
Phone Number:		**Email Address:**	
Assessed Value:		**Sale Price:**	
Inventory Number:		**Condition:**	
Other Details:			
Lost or stolen? ☐ Yes ☐ No	**Date discovered lost/stolen:**		
Date reported to police:		**Police Case Number:**	
Date reported to insurance:		**Insurance Claim Number:**	

FIREARM DETAILS	☐ New ☐ Used		Inventory Number:	
Make/Manufacturer:		Serial Number:		
Model:		Firearm Type:	☐ Pistol ☐ Revolver ☐ Rifle ☐ Shotgun ☐ Muzzle loader/black powder ☐ Air gun ☐ Other	
Importer:		Barrel Length:		
Caliber/Gauge:		NFA item?	☐ Yes ☐ No	
Action:		Curio/Relic?	☐ Yes ☐ No	
Weight:		Sights:		
Ammunition Capacity:		Scope/Rings:		
Stock Type:		Stock Material:		
Other Accessories:		Other identifying marks:		
Alterations:				
Repairs:				
Notes:				
In the event of my death, this firearm should go to:				

This space for images, sketches, other notes, etc.

ACQUISITION DETAILS

Purchased / Acquired From:			Date:	
Address:				
Phone Number:		Email Address:		
Assessed Value:		Purchase Price:		
Inventory Number:		Condition:		
Other Details:				

DISPOSITION DETAILS

Sold / Traded / Gifted / Disposed of to:			Date:	
Address:				
Phone Number:		Email Address:		
Assessed Value:		Sale Price:		
Inventory Number:		Condition:		
Other Details:				

Lost or stolen? ☐ Yes ☐ No	Date discovered lost/stolen:	
Date reported to police:		Police Case Number:
Date reported to insurance:		Insurance Claim Number:

FIREARM DETAILS

☐ New ☐ Used

Make/Manufacturer:		**Inventory Number:**	
		Serial Number:	
Model:		**Firearm Type:**	☐ Pistol ☐ Revolver ☐ Rifle ☐ Shotgun ☐ Muzzle loader/black powder ☐ Air gun ☐ Other
Importer:		**Barrel Length:**	
Caliber/Gauge:		**NFA item?**	☐ Yes ☐ No
Action:		**Curio/Relic?**	☐ Yes ☐ No
Weight:		**Sights:**	
Ammunition Capacity:		**Scope/Rings:**	
Stock Type:		**Stock Material:**	
Other Accessories:		**Other identifying marks:**	
Alterations:			
Repairs:			
Notes:			
In the event of my death, this firearm should go to:			

This space for images, sketches, other notes, etc.

ACQUISITION DETAILS

Purchased / Acquired From:		Date:
Address:		
Phone Number:	Email Address:	
Assessed Value:	Purchase Price:	
Inventory Number:	Condition:	
Other Details:		

DISPOSITION DETAILS

Sold / Traded / Gifted / Disposed of to:		Date:
Address:		
Phone Number:	Email Address:	
Assessed Value:	Sale Price:	
Inventory Number:	Condition:	
Other Details:		
Lost or stolen? ☐ Yes ☐ No	Date discovered lost/stolen:	
Date reported to police:	Police Case Number:	
Date reported to insurance:	Insurance Claim Number:	

FIREARM DETAILS	☐ New ☐ Used	Inventory Number:	
Make/Manufacturer:		Serial Number:	
Model:		Firearm Type:	☐ Pistol ☐ Revolver ☐ Rifle ☐ Shotgun ☐ Muzzle loader/black powder ☐ Air gun ☐ Other
Importer:		Barrel Length:	
Caliber/Gauge:		NFA item?	☐ Yes ☐ No
Action:		Curio/Relic?	☐ Yes ☐ No
Weight:		Sights:	
Ammunition Capacity:		Scope/Rings:	
Stock Type:		Stock Material:	
Other Accessories:		Other identifying marks:	
Alterations:			
Repairs:			
Notes:			
In the event of my death, this firearm should go to:			

This space for images, sketches, other notes, etc.

74

ACQUISITION DETAILS

Purchased / Acquired From:		Date:	
Address:			
Phone Number:		Email Address:	
Assessed Value:		Purchase Price:	
Inventory Number:		Condition:	
Other Details:			

DISPOSITION DETAILS

Sold / Traded / Gifted / Disposed of to:		Date:	
Address:			
Phone Number:		Email Address:	
Assessed Value:		Sale Price:	
Inventory Number:		Condition:	
Other Details:			
Lost or stolen? ☐ Yes ☐ No		Date discovered lost/stolen:	
Date reported to police:		Police Case Number:	
Date reported to insurance:		Insurance Claim Number:	

FIREARM DETAILS

☐ New ☐ Used   Inventory Number:

Make/Manufacturer:		Serial Number:	
Model:		Firearm Type:	☐ Pistol ☐ Revolver ☐ Rifle ☐ Shotgun ☐ Muzzle loader/black powder ☐ Air gun ☐ Other
Importer:		Barrel Length:	
Caliber/Gauge:		NFA item?	☐ Yes ☐ No
Action:		Curio/Relic?	☐ Yes ☐ No
Weight:		Sights:	
Ammunition Capacity:		Scope/Rings:	
Stock Type:		Stock Material:	
Other Accessories:		Other identifying marks:	
Alterations:			
Repairs:			
Notes:			

In the event of my death, this firearm should go to:

This space for images, sketches, other notes, etc.

ACQUISITION DETAILS

Purchased / Acquired From:		Date:	
Address:			
Phone Number:		Email Address:	
Assessed Value:		Purchase Price:	
Inventory Number:		Condition:	
Other Details:			

DISPOSITION DETAILS

Sold / Traded / Gifted / Disposed of to:		Date:	
Address:			
Phone Number:		Email Address:	
Assessed Value:		Sale Price:	
Inventory Number:		Condition:	
Other Details:			
Lost or stolen? ☐ Yes ☐ No	Date discovered lost/stolen:		
Date reported to police:		Police Case Number:	
Date reported to insurance:		Insurance Claim Number:	

FIREARM DETAILS

☐ New   ☐ Used   Inventory Number: _____

Make/Manufacturer:		Serial Number:	
Model:		Firearm Type:	☐ Pistol ☐ Revolver ☐ Rifle ☐ Shotgun ☐ Muzzle loader/black powder ☐ Air gun ☐ Other
Importer:		Barrel Length:	
Caliber/Gauge:		NFA item?	☐ Yes ☐ No
Action:		Curio/Relic?	☐ Yes ☐ No
Weight:		Sights:	
Ammunition Capacity:		Scope/Rings:	
Stock Type:		Stock Material:	
Other Accessories:		Other identifying marks:	
Alterations:			
Repairs:			
Notes:			

In the event of my death, this firearm should go to: _____

This space for images, sketches, other notes, etc.

ACQUISITION DETAILS

Purchased / Acquired From:		Date:	
Address:			
Phone Number:		Email Address:	
Assessed Value:		Purchase Price:	
Inventory Number:		Condition:	
Other Details:			

DISPOSITION DETAILS

Sold / Traded / Gifted / Disposed of to:		Date:	
Address:			
Phone Number:		Email Address:	
Assessed Value:		Sale Price:	
Inventory Number:		Condition:	
Other Details:			

Lost or stolen? ☐ Yes ☐ No	Date discovered lost/stolen:	
Date reported to police:	Police Case Number:	
Date reported to insurance:	Insurance Claim Number:	

FIREARM DETAILS	☐ New ☐ Used	Inventory Number:	
Make/Manufacturer:		Serial Number:	
Model:		Firearm Type:	☐ Pistol ☐ Revolver ☐ Rifle ☐ Shotgun ☐ Muzzle loader/black powder ☐ Air gun ☐ Other
Importer:		Barrel Length:	
Caliber/Gauge:		NFA item?	☐ Yes ☐ No
Action:		Curio/Relic?	☐ Yes ☐ No
Weight:		Sights:	
Ammunition Capacity:		Scope/Rings:	
Stock Type:		Stock Material:	
Other Accessories:		Other identifying marks:	
Alterations:			
Repairs:			
Notes:			
In the event of my death, this firearm should go to:			

This space for images, sketches, other notes, etc.

ACQUISITION DETAILS

Purchased / Acquired From:		**Date:**	
Address:			
Phone Number:		**Email Address:**	
Assessed Value:		**Purchase Price:**	
Inventory Number:		**Condition:**	
Other Details:			

DISPOSITION DETAILS

Sold / Traded / Gifted / Disposed of to:		**Date:**	
Address:			
Phone Number:		**Email Address:**	
Assessed Value:		**Sale Price:**	
Inventory Number:		**Condition:**	
Other Details:			
Lost or stolen? ☐ Yes ☐ No		**Date discovered lost/stolen:**	
Date reported to police:		**Police Case Number:**	
Date reported to insurance:		**Insurance Claim Number:**	

FIREARM DETAILS

☐ New ☐ Used

Make/Manufacturer:	
Model:	
Importer:	
Caliber/Gauge:	
Action:	
Weight:	
Ammunition Capacity:	
Stock Type:	
Other Accessories:	

Inventory Number:

Serial Number:	
Firearm Type:	☐ Pistol ☐ Revolver ☐ Rifle ☐ Shotgun ☐ Muzzle loader/black powder ☐ Air gun ☐ Other
Barrel Length:	
NFA item?	☐ Yes ☐ No
Curio/Relic?	☐ Yes ☐ No
Sights:	
Scope/Rings:	
Stock Material:	
Other identifying marks:	

Alterations:	
Repairs:	
Notes:	

In the event of my death, this firearm should go to:	

This space for images, sketches, other notes, etc.

ACQUISITION DETAILS

Purchased / Acquired From:		Date:	
Address:			
Phone Number:		Email Address:	
Assessed Value:		Purchase Price:	
Inventory Number:		Condition:	
Other Details:			

DISPOSITION DETAILS

Sold / Traded / Gifted / Disposed of to:		Date:	
Address:			
Phone Number:		Email Address:	
Assessed Value:		Sale Price:	
Inventory Number:		Condition:	
Other Details:			
Lost or stolen? ☐ Yes ☐ No		Date discovered lost/stolen:	
Date reported to police:		Police Case Number:	
Date reported to insurance:		Insurance Claim Number:	

FIREARM DETAILS	☐ New ☐ Used	Inventory Number:	
Make/Manufacturer:		Serial Number:	
Model:		Firearm Type:	☐ Pistol ☐ Revolver ☐ Rifle ☐ Shotgun ☐ Muzzle loader/black powder ☐ Air gun ☐ Other
Importer:		Barrel Length:	
Caliber/Gauge:		NFA item?	☐ Yes ☐ No
Action:		Curio/Relic?	☐ Yes ☐ No
Weight:		Sights:	
Ammunition Capacity:		Scope/Rings:	
Stock Type:		Stock Material:	
Other Accessories:		Other identifying marks:	
Alterations:			
Repairs:			
Notes:			
In the event of my death, this firearm should go to:			

This space for images, sketches, other notes, etc.

ACQUISITION DETAILS

Purchased / Acquired From:		Date:	
Address:			
Phone Number:		Email Address:	
Assessed Value:		Purchase Price:	
Inventory Number:		Condition:	
Other Details:			

DISPOSITION DETAILS

Sold / Traded / Gifted / Disposed of to:		Date:	
Address:			
Phone Number:		Email Address:	
Assessed Value:		Sale Price:	
Inventory Number:		Condition:	
Other Details:			
Lost or stolen? ☐ Yes ☐ No		Date discovered lost/stolen:	
Date reported to police:		Police Case Number:	
Date reported to insurance:		Insurance Claim Number:	

FIREARM DETAILS

☐ New   ☐ Used

Make/Manufacturer:		**Serial Number:**	
Model:		**Firearm Type:**	☐ Pistol ☐ Revolver ☐ Rifle ☐ Shotgun ☐ Muzzle loader/black powder ☐ Air gun ☐ Other
Importer:		**Barrel Length:**	
Caliber/Gauge:		**NFA item?**	☐ Yes ☐ No
Action:		**Curio/Relic?**	☐ Yes ☐ No
Weight:		**Sights:**	
Ammunition Capacity:		**Scope/Rings:**	
Stock Type:		**Stock Material:**	
Other Accessories:		**Other identifying marks:**	
Alterations:			
Repairs:			
Notes:			

Inventory Number:

In the event of my death, this firearm should go to:

This space for images, sketches, other notes, etc.

ACQUISITION DETAILS

Purchased / Acquired From:		Date:	
Address:			
Phone Number:		Email Address:	
Assessed Value:		Purchase Price:	
Inventory Number:		Condition:	
Other Details:			

DISPOSITION DETAILS

Sold / Traded / Gifted / Disposed of to:		Date:	
Address:			
Phone Number:		Email Address:	
Assessed Value:		Sale Price:	
Inventory Number:		Condition:	
Other Details:			
Lost or stolen? ☐ Yes ☐ No	Date discovered lost/stolen:		
Date reported to police:		Police Case Number:	
Date reported to insurance:		Insurance Claim Number:	

FIREARM DETAILS	☐ New ☐ Used	Inventory Number:	
Make/Manufacturer:		Serial Number:	
Model:		Firearm Type:	☐ Pistol ☐ Revolver ☐ Rifle ☐ Shotgun ☐ Muzzle loader/black powder ☐ Air gun ☐ Other
Importer:		Barrel Length:	
Caliber/Gauge:		NFA item?	☐ Yes ☐ No
Action:		Curio/Relic?	☐ Yes ☐ No
Weight:		Sights:	
Ammunition Capacity:		Scope/Rings:	
Stock Type:		Stock Material:	
Other Accessories:		Other identifying marks:	
Alterations:			
Repairs:			
Notes:			
In the event of my death, this firearm should go to:			

This space for images, sketches, other notes, etc.

ACQUISITION DETAILS

Purchased / Acquired From:		Date:
Address:		
Phone Number:		Email Address:
Assessed Value:		Purchase Price:
Inventory Number:		Condition:
Other Details:		

DISPOSITION DETAILS

Sold / Traded / Gifted / Disposed of to:		Date:
Address:		
Phone Number:		Email Address:
Assessed Value:		Sale Price:
Inventory Number:		Condition:
Other Details:		

Lost or stolen? ☐ Yes ☐ No	Date discovered lost/stolen:	
Date reported to police:		Police Case Number:
Date reported to insurance:		Insurance Claim Number:

FIREARM DETAILS

FIREARM DETAILS ☐ New ☐ Used	Inventory Number:	

Make/Manufacturer:		Serial Number:	
Model:		Firearm Type:	☐ Pistol ☐ Revolver ☐ Rifle ☐ Shotgun ☐ Muzzle loader/black powder ☐ Air gun ☐ Other
Importer:		Barrel Length:	
Caliber/Gauge:		NFA item?	☐ Yes ☐ No
Action:		Curio/Relic?	☐ Yes ☐ No
Weight:		Sights:	
Ammunition Capacity:		Scope/Rings:	
Stock Type:		Stock Material:	
Other Accessories:		Other identifying marks:	
Alterations:			
Repairs:			
Notes:			

In the event of my death, this firearm should go to:	

This space for images, sketches, other notes, etc.

ACQUISITION DETAILS

Purchased / Acquired From:		**Date:**
Address:		
Phone Number:	**Email Address:**	
Assessed Value:	**Purchase Price:**	
Inventory Number:	**Condition:**	
Other Details:		

DISPOSITION DETAILS

Sold / Traded / Gifted / Disposed of to:		**Date:**
Address:		
Phone Number:	**Email Address:**	
Assessed Value:	**Sale Price:**	
Inventory Number:	**Condition:**	
Other Details:		
Lost or stolen? ☐ Yes ☐ No	**Date discovered lost/stolen:**	
Date reported to police:	**Police Case Number:**	
Date reported to insurance:	**Insurance Claim Number:**	

FIREARM DETAILS ☐ New ☐ Used	Inventory Number:	
Make/Manufacturer:		Serial Number:
Model:		Firearm Type: ☐ Pistol ☐ Revolver ☐ Rifle ☐ Shotgun ☐ Muzzle loader/black powder ☐ Air gun ☐ Other
Importer:		Barrel Length:
Caliber/Gauge:		NFA item? ☐ Yes ☐ No
Action:		Curio/Relic? ☐ Yes ☐ No
Weight:		Sights:
Ammunition Capacity:		Scope/Rings:
Stock Type:		Stock Material:
Other Accessories:		Other identifying marks:
Alterations:		
Repairs:		
Notes:		
In the event of my death, this firearm should go to:		

This space for images, sketches, other notes, etc.

ACQUISITION DETAILS

Purchased / Acquired From:		**Date:**
Address:		
Phone Number:		**Email Address:**
Assessed Value:		**Purchase Price:**
Inventory Number:		**Condition:**
Other Details:		

DISPOSITION DETAILS

Sold / Traded / Gifted / Disposed of to:		**Date:**
Address:		
Phone Number:		**Email Address:**
Assessed Value:		**Sale Price:**
Inventory Number:		**Condition:**
Other Details:		
Lost or stolen? ☐ Yes ☐ No	**Date discovered lost/stolen:**	
Date reported to police:		**Police Case Number:**
Date reported to insurance:		**Insurance Claim Number:**

FIREARM DETAILS

☐ New ☐ Used

Make/Manufacturer:		**Serial Number:**	
Model:		**Firearm Type:**	☐ Pistol ☐ Revolver ☐ Rifle ☐ Shotgun ☐ Muzzle loader/black powder ☐ Air gun ☐ Other
Importer:		**Barrel Length:**	
Caliber/Gauge:		**NFA item?**	☐ Yes ☐ No
Action:		**Curio/Relic?**	☐ Yes ☐ No
Weight:		**Sights:**	
Ammunition Capacity:		**Scope/Rings:**	
Stock Type:		**Stock Material:**	
Other Accessories:		**Other identifying marks:**	
Alterations:			
Repairs:			
Notes:			

Inventory Number:

In the event of my death, this firearm should go to:

This space for images, sketches, other notes, etc.

ACQUISITION DETAILS

Purchased / Acquired From:		Date:
Address:		
Phone Number:	Email Address:	
Assessed Value:	Purchase Price:	
Inventory Number:	Condition:	
Other Details:		

DISPOSITION DETAILS

Sold / Traded / Gifted / Disposed of to:		Date:
Address:		
Phone Number:	Email Address:	
Assessed Value:	Sale Price:	
Inventory Number:	Condition:	
Other Details:		
Lost or stolen? ☐ Yes ☐ No	Date discovered lost/stolen:	
Date reported to police:	Police Case Number:	
Date reported to insurance:	Insurance Claim Number:	

FIREARM DETAILS

☐ New ☐ Used

Inventory Number:	

Make/Manufacturer:		Serial Number:	
Model:		Firearm Type:	☐ Pistol ☐ Revolver ☐ Rifle ☐ Shotgun ☐ Muzzle loader/black powder ☐ Air gun ☐ Other
Importer:		Barrel Length:	
Caliber/Gauge:		NFA item?	☐ Yes ☐ No
Action:		Curio/Relic?	☐ Yes ☐ No
Weight:		Sights:	
Ammunition Capacity:		Scope/Rings:	
Stock Type:		Stock Material:	
Other Accessories:		Other identifying marks:	
Alterations:			
Repairs:			
Notes:			

In the event of my death, this firearm should go to:	

This space for images, sketches, other notes, etc.

ACQUISITION DETAILS

Purchased / Acquired From:		Date:	
Address:			
Phone Number:		Email Address:	
Assessed Value:		Purchase Price:	
Inventory Number:		Condition:	
Other Details:			

DISPOSITION DETAILS

Sold / Traded / Gifted / Disposed of to:		Date:	
Address:			
Phone Number:		Email Address:	
Assessed Value:		Sale Price:	
Inventory Number:		Condition:	
Other Details:			
Lost or stolen? ☐ Yes ☐ No		Date discovered lost/stolen:	
Date reported to police:		Police Case Number:	
Date reported to insurance:		Insurance Claim Number:	

FIREARM DETAILS

☐ New   ☐ Used

Make/Manufacturer:		**Serial Number:**	
Model:		**Firearm Type:**	☐ Pistol ☐ Revolver ☐ Rifle ☐ Shotgun ☐ Muzzle loader/black powder ☐ Air gun ☐ Other
Importer:		**Barrel Length:**	
Caliber/Gauge:		**NFA item?**	☐ Yes ☐ No
Action:		**Curio/Relic?**	☐ Yes ☐ No
Weight:		**Sights:**	
Ammunition Capacity:		**Scope/Rings:**	
Stock Type:		**Stock Material:**	
Other Accessories:		**Other identifying marks:**	
Alterations:			
Repairs:			
Notes:			

Inventory Number:

In the event of my death, this firearm should go to:

This space for images, sketches, other notes, etc.

98

ACQUISITION DETAILS

Purchased / Acquired From:		Date:	
Address:			
Phone Number:		Email Address:	
Assessed Value:		Purchase Price:	
Inventory Number:		Condition:	
Other Details:			

DISPOSITION DETAILS

Sold / Traded / Gifted / Disposed of to:		Date:	
Address:			
Phone Number:		Email Address:	
Assessed Value:		Sale Price:	
Inventory Number:		Condition:	
Other Details:			
Lost or stolen? ☐ Yes ☐ No		Date discovered lost/stolen:	
Date reported to police:		Police Case Number:	
Date reported to insurance:		Insurance Claim Number:	

FIREARM DETAILS

☐ New ☐ Used	**Inventory Number:**	

Make/Manufacturer:		Serial Number:	
Model:		Firearm Type:	☐ Pistol ☐ Revolver ☐ Rifle ☐ Shotgun ☐ Muzzle loader/black powder ☐ Air gun ☐ Other
Importer:		Barrel Length:	
Caliber/Gauge:		NFA item?	☐ Yes ☐ No
Action:		Curio/Relic?	☐ Yes ☐ No
Weight:		Sights:	
Ammunition Capacity:		Scope/Rings:	
Stock Type:		Stock Material:	
Other Accessories:		Other identifying marks:	
Alterations:			
Repairs:			
Notes:			

In the event of my death, this firearm should go to:	

This space for images, sketches, other notes, etc.

ACQUISITION DETAILS

Purchased / Acquired From:		Date:
Address:		
Phone Number:		Email Address:
Assessed Value:		Purchase Price:
Inventory Number:		Condition:
Other Details:		

DISPOSITION DETAILS

Sold / Traded / Gifted / Disposed of to:		Date:
Address:		
Phone Number:		Email Address:
Assessed Value:		Sale Price:
Inventory Number:		Condition:
Other Details:		
Lost or stolen? ☐ Yes ☐ No	Date discovered lost/stolen:	
Date reported to police:		Police Case Number:
Date reported to insurance:		Insurance Claim Number:

FIREARM DETAILS	☐ New ☐ Used	Inventory Number:	
Make/Manufacturer:		Serial Number:	
Model:		Firearm Type:	☐ Pistol ☐ Revolver ☐ Rifle ☐ Shotgun ☐ Muzzle loader/black powder ☐ Air gun ☐ Other
Importer:		Barrel Length:	
Caliber/Gauge:		NFA item?	☐ Yes ☐ No
Action:		Curio/Relic?	☐ Yes ☐ No
Weight:		Sights:	
Ammunition Capacity:		Scope/Rings:	
Stock Type:		Stock Material:	
Other Accessories:		Other identifying marks:	
Alterations:			
Repairs:			
Notes:			
In the event of my death, this firearm should go to:			

This space for images, sketches, other notes, etc.

ACQUISITION DETAILS

Purchased / Acquired From:		Date:
Address:		
Phone Number:		Email Address:
Assessed Value:		Purchase Price:
Inventory Number:		Condition:
Other Details:		

DISPOSITION DETAILS

Sold / Traded / Gifted / Disposed of to:		Date:
Address:		
Phone Number:		Email Address:
Assessed Value:		Sale Price:
Inventory Number:		Condition:
Other Details:		

Lost or stolen? ☐ Yes ☐ No	Date discovered lost/stolen:	
Date reported to police:		Police Case Number:
Date reported to insurance:		Insurance Claim Number:

FIREARM DETAILS	☐ New ☐ Used	Inventory Number:	
Make/Manufacturer:		Serial Number:	
Model:		Firearm Type:	☐ Pistol ☐ Revolver ☐ Rifle ☐ Shotgun ☐ Muzzle loader/black powder ☐ Air gun ☐ Other
Importer:		Barrel Length:	
Caliber/Gauge:		NFA item?	☐ Yes ☐ No
Action:		Curio/Relic?	☐ Yes ☐ No
Weight:		Sights:	
Ammunition Capacity:		Scope/Rings:	
Stock Type:		Stock Material:	
Other Accessories:		Other identifying marks:	
Alterations:			
Repairs:			
Notes:			
In the event of my death, this firearm should go to:			

This space for images, sketches, other notes, etc.

ACQUISITION DETAILS

Purchased / Acquired From:		Date:
Address:		
Phone Number:		Email Address:
Assessed Value:		Purchase Price:
Inventory Number:		Condition:
Other Details:		

DISPOSITION DETAILS

Sold / Traded / Gifted / Disposed of to:		Date:
Address:		
Phone Number:		Email Address:
Assessed Value:		Sale Price:
Inventory Number:		Condition:
Other Details:		

Lost or stolen? ☐ Yes ☐ No		Date discovered lost/stolen:	
Date reported to police:		Police Case Number:	
Date reported to insurance:		Insurance Claim Number:	

FIREARM DETAILS	☐ New	☐ Used	Inventory Number:	
Make/Manufacturer:			Serial Number:	
Model:			Firearm Type:	☐ Pistol ☐ Revolver ☐ Rifle ☐ Shotgun ☐ Muzzle loader/black powder ☐ Air gun ☐ Other
Importer:			Barrel Length:	
Caliber/Gauge:			NFA item?	☐ Yes ☐ No
Action:			Curio/Relic?	☐ Yes ☐ No
Weight:			Sights:	
Ammunition Capacity:			Scope/Rings:	
Stock Type:			Stock Material:	
Other Accessories:			Other identifying marks:	
Alterations:				
Repairs:				
Notes:				
In the event of my death, this firearm should go to:				

This space for images, sketches, other notes, etc.

ACQUISITION DETAILS

Purchased / Acquired From:		Date:
Address:		
Phone Number:		Email Address:
Assessed Value:		Purchase Price:
Inventory Number:		Condition:
Other Details:		

DISPOSITION DETAILS

Sold / Traded / Gifted / Disposed of to:		Date:
Address:		
Phone Number:		Email Address:
Assessed Value:		Sale Price:
Inventory Number:		Condition:
Other Details:		
Lost or stolen? ☐ Yes ☐ No	Date discovered lost/stolen:	
Date reported to police:		Police Case Number:
Date reported to insurance:		Insurance Claim Number:

Notes

Notes

Notes

Notes

Secondary Index

Grouping Type (Ex: Make, Type, Action Type, etc)	Make/Model	Inventory Number	Page Number

Secondary Index

Grouping Type (Ex: Make, Type, Action Type, etc)	Make/Model	Inventory Number	Page Number

Secondary Index

Grouping Type (Ex: Make, Type, Action Type, etc)	Make/Model	Inventory Number	Page Number

Secondary Index

Grouping Type (Ex: Make, Type, Action Type, etc)	Make/Model	Inventory Number	Page Number

Secondary Index

Grouping Type (Ex: Make, Type, Action Type, etc)	Make/Model	Inventory Number	Page Number

Secondary Index

Grouping Type (Ex: Make, Type, Action Type, etc)	Make/Model	Inventory Number	Page Number

Made in the USA
Middletown, DE
07 January 2023

21638339R00066